BEYOND THE ABSENT FATHER

Beyond the absent father

TABLE OF CONTENTS

Beyond the absent father

INTRODUCTION

The abandonment of one or both parents can be a painful and traumatic event in a person's life. It can affect self-esteem, interpersonal relationships, and overall emotional well-being. Abandonment can occur in a number of ways, such as parental separation, the death of one of the parents, or emotional or physical neglect. In either case, it can leave a person feeling alone, insecure, and without a sense of belonging.

It is important to recognize that the abandonment is not the fault of the abandoned person. Parents have a responsibility to care for and protect their children, and when they fail to do so, it is a failure of their behavior, not their child's. However, this does not mean that it is easy to overcome abandonment. It can take time and effort to work through your emotions and find peace.

One of the first things a person can do to begin the healing process is to acknowledge and accept their feelings. It is important to allow yourself to feel the sadness, anger, frustration, and any other emotions that come up, rather than suppress or deny them. Talking with friends, family, or a therapist can help you process these emotions and feel heard and supported.

It is also helpful to understand the reasons behind the abandonment, if possible. Although this does not excuse the parent's behavior, it can help to see things from a broader perspective and understand that the abandonment was not the fault of the abandoned person. This can also help release some of the anger or resentment felt towards the parents.

Another important thing is to seek emotional support. Do not isolate yourself in feelings of abandonment, as this can make things worse. Seeking help from friends, family, therapists, or support groups can provide a safe space to process feelings and receive needed support.

Also, it is important to work on forgiveness. Forgiving parents does not mean forgetting or justifying their behavior, but rather letting go of the anger and resentment they may have towards them. This can be difficult, but it can be a crucial part of the healing process.

It is important to remember that abandonment is not the fault of the abandoned person. One should not blame oneself for the actions of the parents. It is crucial to work on self-esteem and self-confidence in order to overcome feelings of abandonment and build a positive life.

Finding a purpose in life can also be helpful. This can be a career, hobby, or volunteering. By finding something that provides a sense of meaning and purpose, self-esteem and a sense of belonging can be enhanced.

ACKNOWLEDGE AND ACCEPT YOUR FEELINGS

Acknowledging and accepting your feelings is crucial to overcome paternal or maternal abandonment and find inner peace. When you experience feelings of abandonment, hurt, sadness, and anger, it is important to allow yourself to feel these emotions rather than repress or deny them.

Sometimes it can be hard to acknowledge and accept your feelings. You may feel ashamed, vulnerable, or fearful when expressing your emotions. However, it is important to remember that it is normal to feel this way after a traumatic experience such as abandonment.

Denial of your feelings can make the situation worse. Suppressed feelings can manifest in negative ways, such as anxiety, depression, and anger. Therefore, it is essential to express your feelings in a healthy way.

Talking with trusted friends and family can be a great way to express your feelings. People close to you can provide emotional support and can help you feel understood and accepted. If you don't feel comfortable talking to your friends or family, consider seeking professional help.

A therapist can help you process your feelings more deeply and find ways to deal with your emotions. Therapists can provide you with tools and techniques to manage your feelings more effectively.

It's also important to remember that not everyone will be comfortable talking about parental abandonment. Some people may not understand your feelings or may not know how to help you. If this happens, don't give up. Find someone who can understand and support you.

Besides talking with friends, family, or a therapist, there are other ways to express your feelings. You can write your feelings in a journal or express them through art, music, or movement. These creative forms of expression can help you release your feelings in a healthy way.

Remember that acknowledging and accepting your feelings doesn't mean you have to hold on to them forever. As you process your emotions, you may feel ready to release them and move on.

Learning to accept and express your feelings can be a challenging process, but it is an important step in overcoming parental abandonment and finding inner peace. By acknowledging and accepting your feelings, you can free yourself from the emotional baggage you've been carrying and move toward a healthier, happier life.

UNDERSTAND THE REASONS BEHIND ABANDONMENT

Understanding the reasons behind abandonment can be a difficult task, but it is an important part of the healing process. Trying to understand why your parents made the decision to leave you can help you see things in a bigger perspective and accept the situation.

It is important to note that understanding the reasons behind abandonment does not mean justifying your behavior. Abandonment is an unfair and hurtful act that can have lasting effects on a person's life. However, understanding the reasons behind the abandonment can help you find inner peace and heal your emotional wounds.

The reasons behind abandonment can vary. Sometimes parents may have made the decision to abandon their children due to personal problems, such as mental illness, substance abuse, or lack of financial resources. At other times, they may have been forced to abandon their children due to circumstances beyond their control, such as war, immigration, or death.

It is important to remember that the reason behind the abandonment does not change the fact that you have been abandoned. However, understanding the reasons behind the abandonment can help you stop blaming yourself or your parents and find ways to move forward.

It may be helpful to talk with other family members or close friends to gain information about the circumstances surrounding the abandonment. If you don't have access to this information, you may want to talk to a therapist for help in understanding the reasons behind the abandonment.

Once you understand the reasons behind the abandonment, it's important to remember that you are not responsible for your parents' behavior. You can find ways to move forward and build a satisfying life without depending on them.

It is important to remember that healing from abandonment does not happen overnight. It is a process that takes time and effort. However, understanding the reasons behind the abandonment can be an important first step towards healing.

Remember that you are not alone in your fight against abandonment. There are many resources and support communities available to help you overcome emotional pain and find inner peace. You can look for support groups online or in your local area to connect with people who have been through similar experiences.

Ultimately, understanding the reasons behind the abandonment can help you free yourself from the emotional baggage and find the strength and confidence to build the life you want.

Beyond the absent father

SEEK SUPPORT

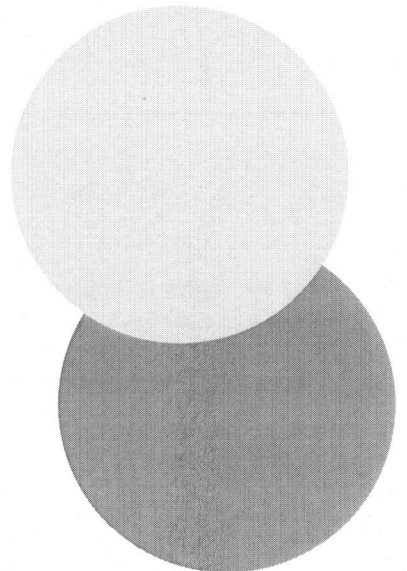

When you have experienced parental abandonment, it can be very difficult to deal with the feelings of hurt, sadness, and abandonment that can arise. One of the most important ways to get through this type of experience is to seek emotional support. Do not isolate yourself in your feelings, seek help from friends, family, therapists or support groups. Here are some ways seeking support can help you find inner peace:

Emotional Expression: The process of talking to someone about your feelings can help you process and deal with them effectively. It's important that you find people you can trust so that you can talk freely about your emotions without fear of being judged.

Feeling Understood: When you meet someone who has been through a similar experience as you, you can feel understood and supported. Find support groups online or in your local community to connect with people who have experienced parental abandonment.

Feeling like you're not alone: Seeking support can help you feel like you're not alone in your abandonment experience. It can be very comforting to know that there are other people who are going through the same thing as you and who are willing to support you.

Professional help: If you feel like you need more help than you can get from friends and family, consider seeking professional help from a therapist. A therapist can help you process your feelings and find effective ways to deal with them.

Practical advice: When you seek support, you can get practical advice on how to deal with your emotions and find peace. People who have been through similar experiences may have valuable insights into dealing with abandonment and finding ways to move forward.

Strengthen relationships: Seeking support can also help you strengthen relationships with people who support you. It can be an opportunity to connect with friends and family in a deeper and more meaningful way.

Breaking Isolation: When you experience parental or maternal abandonment, you may feel isolated from others. Seeking support is an effective way to break that isolation and connect with people who can help you.

Understand your feelings: When you talk to someone about your feelings, it can help you better understand why you feel a certain way. Understanding your feelings is an important part of the healing process.

Learn from others: Seeking support can also be an opportunity to learn from the experiences of others. You can gain new perspectives on how to deal with abandonment and find ways to move forward.

Finding peace: Ultimately, seeking support can help you find the inner peace you need to move forward after parental abandonment. With the right time and support, you can move past emotional pain and find a fulfilling and meaningful life.

FORGIVE YOUR
PARENTS

When it comes to getting over parental abandonment, it can be hard to forgive your parents for what they put you through. However, forgiveness is an important part of the emotional healing process and can help you find the inner peace you need to move on. Here are some ways forgiveness can help you:

Emotional release: Forgiveness can release you from the anger and resentment you may feel toward your parents. When you get rid of these negative emotions, you can feel a sense of relief and inner peace.

Empathy: Forgiving your parents can help you develop a deeper understanding of why they made the decision to abandon you. It can help you see things from their perspective and understand their reasons.

Emotional Healing: Forgiveness is an important part of the emotional healing process after parental abandonment. It can help you release any emotional pain you may be feeling and find ways to move forward.

Guilt Release: When you forgive your parents, you can also release any guilt you may feel about the situation. You can realize that it wasn't your fault and that you didn't do anything wrong.

Strengthening the relationship: forgiving your parents can help you strengthen the relationship with them. It can be an opportunity to connect in a deeper and more meaningful way.

Inner Peace: When you let go of grudges and anger, you can feel a sense of inner peace that allows you to move forward and find happiness.

Acceptance: Forgiveness can also help you accept the situation and stop fighting it. You may realize that you cannot change the past, but you can control your emotional response to it.

Shame release: Parental abandonment can make you feel ashamed and stigmatized. Forgiveness can help you free yourself from this shame and find confidence in yourself.

Personal Strengthening: Forgiving your parents can also be a way to strengthen yourself personally. You can prove to yourself that you are capable of overcoming difficult situations and finding inner peace.

Openness to new experiences: When you forgive your parents, you may also be more open to new experiences and relationships. You can move past the hurt and anger and move towards a more positive and exciting future.

Forgiving your parents is not easy, but it is an important part of the emotional healing process after parental abandonment. Forgiveness does not mean forgetting or justifying your parents' behavior, but letting go of any anger and resentment you may have toward them. Forgiveness can help you release negative emotions, find inner peace, and move toward a more positive and exciting future.

DO NOT BLAME
YOURSELF

When a father or mother abandons their child, it is normal for the child to feel confused, betrayed and abandoned. Often the person who has been abandoned may blame themselves and wonder what they did wrong to deserve such treatment. It is important to remember that the abandonment is not the child's fault and that there is nothing the child has done to deserve to be abandoned.

Sometimes people who have been dumped may experience feelings of abandonment and rejection in other relationships throughout their lives. They may be afraid to trust people, or they may feel like they are being abandoned again if someone walks away from them. It is important to work on these feelings in order to have healthy and happy relationships in the future.

One way to overcome abandonment is to learn to love and care for yourself . This can include taking care of your body and mind, having hobbies and activities you enjoy, and surrounding yourself with people who support you and love you for who you are.

Abandonment can also have an impact on a person's self-esteem and confidence. It is important to remember that you are valuable and worthy of love and respect. Learn to recognize your strengths and abilities and work on those areas in which you would like to improve.

If you feel caught up in your feelings of abandonment, it may help to seek help from a therapist. A therapist can help you process your emotions and develop strategies to overcome abandonment and find peace.

In some cases, it may be useful to find contact with the father or mother who abandoned you. However, this can be difficult and may not be appropriate for everyone. If you decide to seek contact, it is important to do so for the right reasons and not out of an obligation to maintain a relationship with your parents.

Remember that overcoming abandonment is not something that happens overnight. It is a process that can take time and effort. But over time, it is possible to find peace and happiness after abandonment.

It is important to accept that we cannot control the actions of others, including our parents. We can work on our own growth and well-being, and ultimately it is our own happiness and well-being that matters.

Don't feel obligated to maintain a relationship with your parents if it does you more harm than good. Sometimes it is necessary to set healthy boundaries to protect your own mental and emotional health.

Finally, remember that abandonment does not define who you are. You are more than the person who has been abandoned. You are a valuable person, worthy of love and respect, and you deserve to live a happy and fulfilling life.

LEARN TO TAKE CARE OF YOURSELF

Learning to take care of yourself is essential to overcome paternal or maternal abandonment and find inner peace. Self-care can help you stay healthy both physically and emotionally and can improve your self-esteem and self-confidence. Here are some ways you can take care of yourself:

Practice meditation: Meditation is an effective technique for reducing stress and anxiety, and it can help you find inner peace. Take a few minutes a day to meditate and connect with yourself.

Exercise regularly: Exercise is not only good for your body, but also for your mind. Exercise regularly to release endorphins and improve your mood.

Get enough sleep: Sleep is essential for maintaining good physical and mental health. Make sure you get at least 7-8 hours of sleep a day so that your body and mind can rest and recover.

Eat healthy foods: Healthy eating can help you keep your body and mind fit. Be sure to include a variety of nutritious foods in your diet, such as fruits, vegetables, lean protein, and healthy fats.

Do something you enjoy: Spend time doing something that you enjoy and that makes you feel good about yourself. It can be anything from reading a book to doing crafts or going for a walk.

Set Healthy Boundaries: Set healthy boundaries in your relationships to protect yourself from toxic or negative situations that may affect your emotional well-being.

Practice gratitude: Focus on the positive things in your life and practice gratitude. Make a list of the things you are grateful for and read that list when you need a positive boost.

Get therapy: Therapy can be a useful tool to help you process your emotions and overcome parental abandonment. A therapist can help you work through your feelings and develop healthy coping skills.

Spend time with friends and family: Surrounding yourself with people who support you and make you feel good can improve your emotional well-being and help you find inner peace.

CREATE A SOOTHING AMBIANCE: Create a relaxing environment in your home or personal space. You can add candles, plants, or soft music to help you feel more calm and at peace.

Beyond the absent father

WORK ON YOUR SELF-ESTEEM

Paternal or maternal abandonment can significantly affect a person's self-esteem. It is common for children who are abandoned by their parents to feel rejected and unwanted, which can lower their self-esteem. However, it is important to remember that abandonment is not the child's fault and does not define their value as a person.

One way to work on your self-esteem after abandonment is to focus on your strengths and abilities. Identify what you are good at doing and spend time cultivating those skills. You can look for opportunities to improve your skills through courses, workshops or by practicing at home. This will help you feel more confident and proud of yourself.

It is also important to practice self-compassion. Instead of being critical of yourself, try to be kind and compassionate. Acknowledge that you have been through trauma and give yourself permission to feel sad or angry. Try to treat yourself with the same compassion and care that you would a friend.

Another way to work on your self-esteem is to surround yourself with people who support you and make you feel valued. Find friends and family who support you in your goals and encourage you to be your best self. If you feel lonely or isolated, consider joining a support group or finding a therapist to help you work through your feelings and emotions.

Also, it's important to set healthy boundaries. Often, people who have been abandoned by their parents can have trouble setting healthy boundaries in relationships. They may be afraid of being abandoned again or may allow others to treat them badly because they don't feel worthy of love and respect. Working on your boundaries will help you establish healthier and more positive relationships.

You may need to work on conflict resolution and communication as well. If you're having trouble expressing yourself or solving problems, consider taking classes or joining a social skills group to improve your skills in these areas. This will help you have more satisfying relationships and feel more confident about yourself.

Remember that self-esteem is not built overnight and that it is a constant process. Work on your strengths, set healthy boundaries, and surround yourself with supportive people. Be kind and compassionate to yourself and remember that you are valuable and worthy of love and respect.

CREATE MEANINGFUL
NEW RELATIONSHIPS

Abandonment, whether by one parent or both, can leave a lasting mark on a person. You may feel abandoned, unwanted, or undeserving of love. However, it is important that you know that you are not alone and that there are many people who have gone through the same thing and have found ways to overcome it.

Creating meaningful new relationships is one of the ways to overcome abandonment. These relationships can be with friends, partner or a community. By building meaningful relationships, you can find a sense of belonging and connection with others that will help you heal. It is important that you take the time to meet new people and establish positive relationships in your life.

It is possible that after the abandonment, you have difficulty trusting others. It's normal for you to feel this way, but don't let this stop you from creating new relationships. Start by making slow, deep connections with people who share your interests and values. You can join groups or clubs that share your hobbies or interests, which can make it easier to meet new people.

Meaningful relationships don't always have to be with people. You can make connections with animals, nature, or even a creative activity. These relationships can provide comfort and emotional support, which can be especially beneficial for those who have a hard time trusting people.

When establishing new meaningful relationships, it's important to be authentic and vulnerable. Don't be afraid to share your feelings and thoughts with the people who care about you. Vulnerability can be difficult, but it is essential to building lasting and meaningful relationships.

Remember that creating meaningful new relationships takes time and effort. Don't expect to find friends or a partner overnight, and don't be discouraged if you don't feel connected to people right away. Keep working on building positive and meaningful relationships in your life and you will see how this helps you overcome abandonment.

In addition to building new relationships, it is important that you work on yourself. If you have experienced abandonment, you may have developed self-esteem and confidence issues. To work on your self-esteem, start by recognizing your qualities and abilities. Make a list of the things you like about yourself and the things you have accomplished in life. As you learn to value your own qualities and abilities, you will feel more secure and confident in yourself.

Another way to work on your self-esteem is through self-expression. Find a way to express yourself that makes you feel good about yourself, like writing, drawing, or dancing. Self-expression allows you to process your emotions and feelings in a healthy and positive way.

It is also important that you give yourself permission to make mistakes and fail. Accepting that you can't always be perfect will allow you to be more compassionate and kind to yourself. As you learn to accept and love yourself, you will feel more secure and confident in yourself.

Beyond the absent father

DO NOT GIVE UP

Overcoming paternal or maternal abandonment is a process that takes time and effort. It is important to remember that there is no single or easy solution, but there are many strategies you can implement to help you find peace. One of the main tips is not to give up, as the process can be difficult and painful, but in the end it is possible to find peace and healing.

Another important tip is to seek professional help if necessary. A therapist can help you better understand your feelings and emotions, and provide you with tools and strategies to deal with them in healthy ways. They can also help you process and understand events from the past and how they have affected your life today.

Also, it is important to remember that you are not alone. Abandonment is a common problem and there are many people who have gone through similar experiences. Finding support groups or online communities can be a great way to connect with others who have been through similar experiences and can provide emotional support.

Another helpful strategy is to find healthy ways to express your emotions. Writing, art, or music can be effective ways to process your feelings and release negative emotions. It is also important to allow yourself to feel your emotions without judging yourself and without repressing them.

It is important to remember that abandonment is not your fault, and you should not feel responsible for your parents' behaviors. Work on forgiving them, not for what they did, but for yourself, so that you can let go of any anger and resentment you may feel.

Another important tip is to work on your self-esteem and self-confidence. Abandonment can affect your self-esteem and make you feel insecure or unloved. Practicing self-care and doing activities that make you feel good about yourself, like exercising, reading, or meditating, can be a great way to boost your self-esteem and find inner peace.

Also, it is important to create new meaningful relationships. Building healthy, meaningful relationships with friends, a partner, or a community can provide you with support and love, helping you overcome feelings of abandonment. Make sure that you surround yourself with positive and loving people who will support you on your journey to healing.

Overcoming paternal or maternal abandonment is not easy, but it is possible. Seek help if necessary, work on forgiving yourself and your parents, work on your self-esteem and self-confidence, and create new meaningful relationships. Do not give up on your path to peace and healing.

TALK WITH YOUR PARENTS

Talking to your parents can be an important step in the process of overcoming parental abandonment. However, it is important to keep in mind that this conversation can be difficult, and you may not resolve all of your feelings in one conversation. Here are some tips that can help you have an effective conversation with your parents:

Choose a suitable time: Choose a time when your parents are available and calm to talk. Avoid talking when they are stressed or angry.

Be clear and honest: explain your feelings and how the abandonment has affected you. Be honest, but don't make accusations or blame your parents.

Listen to their response: allow them to talk and explain their side of the story. Try to listen without judging.

Ask questions: If you're not sure about something, ask questions to clear up any misunderstandings.

Be respectful: Treat your parents with respect and compassion. Do not speak negatively or insultingly.

Don't expect an apology: While it would be nice to get an apology from your parents, you may not get one. Don't expect an apology as a condition of feeling better.

Set limits: If the conversation becomes too intense or difficult, set limits and agree to continue the conversation at another time.

Consider family therapy: If you feel the discussion hasn't helped, consider seeking family therapy to continue working on the relationship.

Accept their limitations: Your parents may have limitations in their ability to understand or change their behavior. Accept this and work on your own healing.

Be compassionate with yourself: Talking to your parents can be an important step, but it's not a magic bullet. Be compassionate with yourself and give yourself time to process your feelings.

SEEK A PURPOSE

When a person has experienced the abandonment of a father or mother, it is common for them to feel lost and meaningless in life. Therefore, an important strategy to overcome abandonment is to find a purpose in life. Purpose can be a source of motivation, a reason to get up in the morning and keep going even when the going gets tough.

Finding a purpose doesn't mean you have to have a successful career or do something extraordinary. It's about finding something that makes you feel good about yourself and gives you a sense of accomplishment. This can be anything from learning a new language to dedicating yourself to a social cause. The important thing is that you feel committed and passionate about it.

Purpose can also help you build a strong and cohesive identity. By establishing a purpose in life, you can begin to define yourself in positive terms and create a personal narrative that helps you understand who you are and what you aspire to.

One way to find purpose is to explore your interests and passions. Think about the things that make you happy, the topics you are passionate about, or the values that are important to you. You can also look for volunteer opportunities, practice a sport or physical activity, take classes online or in person, among other things.

Another way to find purpose is by setting clear goals and objectives. This will give you a sense of direction and a plan to work towards something meaningful. It's important to set realistic and measurable goals, and celebrate every little accomplishment along the way.

Remember that finding a purpose does not happen overnight. Take the time you need to explore and experiment. If you're not sure what you're passionate about, keep trying new things until you find something that makes you feel good.

Finding a purpose is an effective way to overcome abandonment and find inner peace. It helps you build a strong identity, set goals and objectives, and find a reason to get up every day. It can be anything that makes you feel passionate and committed, and the important thing is that it makes you feel good about yourself.

BE KIND TO YOURSELF

Being kind to yourself is crucial to overcoming abandonment and finding peace. It can be easy to fall into the trap of being overly self-critical and blaming yourself for your parent's abandonment. However, this only makes things worse and prevents you from moving towards healing and recovery.

Learn to be kind to yourself by remembering that the abandonment was not your fault. It is important to recognize that you had no control over your parents' decision and that there is nothing you can do to change the past. Don't blame yourself for something that was out of your control.

Also, it is important that you give yourself permission to feel your emotions and take the time to process them. Don't pressure yourself to "get over" the abandonment quickly. Give yourself the time and space you need to process your emotions and heal.

Another way to be kind to yourself is to take care of your physical and emotional well-being. Do things that make you feel good about yourself, like exercising, getting enough sleep, eating right, and taking care of your mental health. Don't force yourself to do things you don't like or feel uncomfortable just because you think you should.

Learning to accept yourself is also part of being kind to yourself. Learn to love and accept your strengths and weaknesses. Work on your self-esteem and self-confidence, and don't let abandonment make you feel less valuable or worthy of love and happiness.

Try to cultivate a positive mindset and gratitude in your life. Instead of focusing on what you lack, try to focus on what you have and the things you are grateful for. Practice meditation or mindfulness to help you find calm and mental clarity.

Finally, don't be afraid to ask for help if you need it. Seek support from friends, family, therapists, or support groups. Sometimes talking to someone who has been through similar experiences can be very helpful. Remember that you are not alone and that there are people willing to support you on your path to healing and inner peace.

CONCLUSION

Overcoming abandonment is a complex
process that requires time, patience,
and emotional support. Accept and
process feelings related to
abandonment, seek help from friends,
family, therapists or support groups,
forgive parents, not blame yourself,
take care of yourself, work on your
self-esteem, create new meaningful
relationships, do not giving up,
talking to your parents, and finding a
purpose in life are some of the steps
you can take to overcome abandonment
and find peace.

It is important to remember that there
is no single solution to overcome
abandonment, and that the recovery
process can be different for each
person. Some people may be able to get
over giving up more quickly than
others, but the important thing is to
focus on progress, not perfection.

Also, it is essential to keep in mind
that the recovery process does not mean

that you should forget or justify your parents' behavior. Forgiveness is an important part of the healing process, but it does not mean that you have to accept or allow any harmful behavior in the future. It is important to set healthy boundaries and protect yourself from future situations that may be harmful.

Finally, it is important to remember that seeking professional help is not a sign of weakness, but rather a show of strength and courage in recognizing that you need help to overcome abandonment. Therapists can provide specific tools and techniques to help you overcome the emotional challenges associated with abandonment.

Overcoming abandonment can be a difficult process, but it is possible to find peace and happiness in the long run. Taking active steps to process feelings, seeking emotional support help, working on your self-esteem, creating new meaningful relationships, finding purpose in life, and not giving up are some of the steps you can take to overcome abandonment and find peace. Remember that you are not alone in this process and that help is always available for those who seek it.

Manufactured by Amazon.ca
Acheson, AB